Hey Kids! Let's Visit New York City

Teresa Mills

Life Experiences Publishing

Bluff City, Tennessee

Teresa Mills/Life Experiences Publishing
PO Box 53
Bluff City, TN 37618
kid-friendly-family-vacations.com

Book Layout © 2014 BookDesignTemplates.com

Hey Kids! Let's Visit New York City/ Teresa Mills -- 1st ed.
ISBN-13: 978-1-946049-06-3

Contents

Preface

Welcome

New York City is a fascinating place to visit and can be an especially fun place to visit with kids.
There are a lot of parks and places to take time out to relax. There are a lot of historical places to visit and learn. And there is a lot of shopping and restaurants to have fun!

This book includes some history, interspersed with fun facts about the things to do in New York City.

You can use this book to visit New York City right from your own home! You will enjoy this book if you are preparing for a trip to NYC with the family and want to learn more about it, if you are writing a report for school, or if you just want to enjoy the book and pictures for fun.

I hope you enjoy this book and use it to learn a little more about this great city.

When you are ready to take your family vacation in New York City, I have a free gift for you!

http://kid-friendly-family-vacations.com/nycattractions

Also, take advantage of our companion activity and coloring books to complement this book... available as a set and separately.

https://kid-friendly-family-vacations.com/nycpkg

When you have completed this book, I invite you to enjoy the other books in the series. We visit Washington DC, a Cruise Ship, London England, San Francisco, Savannah Georgia, Paris France, and Charleston South Carolina.

Enjoy!

Teresa Mills

1

The Empire State Building

The Empire State Building is one of the most popular landmarks in the whole world. It is also one of the most romanticized. Thanks to a number of movies filmed in the skyscraper, the Empire State Building has become one of the places to go to for lovers and families alike.

William F. Lamb designed the Empire State Building. He produced the design drawings in just two weeks because the firm he worked for (Shreve, Lamb, and Harmon) had already designed the Reynolds Building in Winston-Salem, North Carolina and the Carew Tower in Cincinnati, Ohio.

The Empire State Building

Did you know that the Empire State Building used to be the tallest building in the world? It held that distinction from 1931 to 1972 for a total of forty-one years. Even though other skyscrapers have sprouted and dwarfed the 1,250-feet-tall (1,454 feet to the top of the spire) Empire State Building, it remains one of the most majestic man-made wonders in history.

Located in the heart of Manhattan, the Empire State Building has 103 floors, 1,872 steps, 73 elevators, and 6,514 windows. Imagine how much work the window cleaners have on their hands!

On the 86th floor is an observation deck where most of the tourists flock. The same can be said of the observation deck on the 102nd floor. It's a good thing the decks are strong since around four million people go there each year.

Fun Facts About The Empire State Building

- A race is held annually where the competitors must climb up to the 86th floor. That's a total of 1,576 steps. Whew!
- The lightning rod perched on top of the building attracts lighting at an average of twenty-three strikes per year.
- The Empire State Building is considered the most photographed building in the world. This was determined by a group of researchers from Cornell University who studied Flickr photos numbering in the millions.
- Every year, the staff of the Empire State Building send a Father's Day card to the staff of the Reynolds Building in Winston-Salem, North Carolina to recognize its role as the predecessor of the Empire State Building.

2

The Statue of Liberty

What comes to mind when you hear the words "New York City"? For many, the Statue of Liberty will quickly come to mind.

The Statue of Liberty is known as Lady Liberty. Did you realize that the Lady Liberty has a longer name? This dignified woman's full name is Liberty Enlightening the World.

The Statue of Liberty is one of the most enduring and most important symbols of the United States and New York City in particular. Even though the statue is in America, Americans did not build this towering beauty. Do you know who built the statue? The US owes her Lady Liberty to the French, particularly to Edouard de Laboulaye and Frederic-Auguste Bartholdi.

The Statue of Liberty

It was Laboulaye's idea for France to present their American friends with the best gift ever. Weighing 450,000 pounds and reaching a height of 93 meters (from the ground to the tip of the Lady's torch), the Statue of Liberty is the heaviest — if not the greatest — gift the Americans have received. And no, it didn't come in a humongous box with a mile-long ribbon. It did, however, come in hundreds of crates. The French, led by one of the world's greatest sculptors in Bartholdi, took nine years to finish the statue. Once they were done, they shipped the statue piece by big piece in a total of 214 crates. They then built the statue on the former Bedloe Island, now known as Liberty

Island, since all ships arriving in New York pass by
the island.

The Statue of Liberty from a tour boat

The Lady has seen countless people who want to peek out of the twenty-five windows in her crown. With an average of four million visitors each year, more than a hundred million people have visited this magnificent landmark already. And did you realize that the statue was not always green, as it is right now? It is actually made of copper but turned green because of oxidation from all the seawater evaporating around it.

Fun Facts About The Statue of Liberty

- Lady Liberty's sandals measure twenty-five feet long. That makes her a size 879!
- The crown worn by Lady Liberty has seven spikes signifying the seven continents or the seven oceans in the world.
- Filmmakers have a thing for destroying Lady Liberty. In movies such as *The Day After Tomorrow* and *Independence Day*, the statue was seen being destroyed or having already fallen.

3

Rockefeller Center

Do you realize why West 49th Street and 5th Avenue is one of the most popular addresses in New York? That's because the popular Rockefeller Center can be found there. Named after John D. Rockefeller, Jr., this tourist attraction was named a National Historic Landmark in 1987.

The holiday season in New York City is one splendid spectacle after another. You have the much-anticipated Ball Drop (on New Year's Eve) at Times Square, and then there's the traditional Christmas tree at the Rockefeller Center. The gigantic Rockefeller Christmas Tree, which is usually an actual Norway spruce and not just some plastic tree, measures at least sixty-five feet tall but often reaches seventy-five feet. Can you imagine how high that is? Put five cars, one in front of another bumper to bumper, and then raise them up. That's a safe estimate how high the tree is. But that's just the average tree — the tallest ever Rockefeller Christmas Tree reached 100 feet!

The Christmas Tree in Rockefeller Center

There are 200 flagpoles that line the plaza at street level. These flag poles display the flags of the United Nations member countries, the US States and territories, or decorative flags for seasonal events.

A view upward from Rockefeller Center

Fun Facts About Rockefeller Center

- The ice-skating rink in front of the Christmas tree was launched in 1936.
- Gamers will surely love visiting the Nintendo World Store at 10 Rockefeller Plaza.
- The star that sits at the top of the Rockefeller Christmas tree measures nine and a half feet wide and weighs 550 pounds.
- The Rockefeller Center is the home of numerous talk shows and other TV shows, from past to present. Some of them include *The Tonight Show*, the defunct *Late Night with Conan O'Brien*, and *Saturday Night Live*.

4

Top of the Rock Observatory

Top of the Rock is an observation deck on top of the Rockefeller Center. The building where the Top of the Rock Observation Deck sits is officially known as the General Electric Building.

The public was first allowed on the observation deck in 1933, but it was closed for renovation from 1986 to 2005. It took around nineteen years and $75 million for the deck to be renovated. Once operations resumed, people got a much better experience and view of New York City.

While on the deck, you get a great view of the Brooklyn Bridge, Central Park and the Chrysler Building, especially during the day. At night the view is also spectacular, especially with the Empire State Building's majestic height and lights. The best time to visit is right before sunset so you can enjoy both views during daytime and nighttime. You can also go during the day and come back at night by purchasing the Sunrise/Sunset tickets.

Viewer at the Top of the Rock Observatory

One of the highlights of your visit to the deck is the ride to get there. Have you ever ridden an elevator where you can see all the gears and gadgets that pulls it up? Well, with this one you can. The ceiling of the elevator is made of see-through glass, allowing you a peek at the elevator's mechanism. Some images that depict the building's rich history are also projected on the transparent ceiling.

Fun Facts About Top of the Rock

- There's an ongoing debate on which is better — the Top of the Rock or the Empire State Building's   observation deck. Of course, both landmarks are places you must visit, but one thing that sets the Rock apart is that you can take a selfie with the Empire State behind you.
- Do you know what the GE Building is more popularly known as? If you watch TV, you may have heard of the sitcom called 30 Rock. That's the building's nickname, which comes from its address 30 Rockefeller Plaza.
- The observation deck is laid out to resemble the deck of on ocean liner, so you get a bird's eye view of the city.

5

Central Park

Who would have thought that there is an urban park in New York City? When you think of New York City, what almost always comes to mind are the skyscrapers and the overcrowded Times Square. This is why the city is known as a "concrete jungle". But lo and behold, there are still places in the city that are green. Central Park is one of them.

New York City's Central Park, located smack in the middle of Manhattan, is the first ever public landscaped park in the United States. Work on Central Park commenced in 1857 and ended in 1873, taking 15 years to complete the project. It covers 843 acres which is around three and a half square miles. It contains seven bodies of water, 25,000 trees (including 1,700 American elms), and thirty-six arches and bridges.

Central Park

Aside from the trees and plants all around, Central Park is also home to different species of birds and other animals. This is a great place to relax and enjoy nature, even if it was man-made. Other man-made wonders found in the park are sculptures, monuments, fountains (particularly the Angel of the Waters), and other artworks.

But Central Park is not just about plants, trees, and animals! You can have fun in any of the more than twenty playgrounds in the park. You can also practice your swing and strokes in the park's handball courts and baseball fields.

Angel of the Waters Fountain in Central Park

If you are a music lover, the Great Lawn is where different musicians and artists perform. The New York Philharmonic Orchestra is a regular performer, while stars such as Simon and Garfunkel and Barbra Streisand have held concerts here.

Fun Facts About Central Park

- The design of the park was the result of a contest conducted in 1858. The Greensward Plan of Frederick Law Olmstead and Calvert Vaux won over other designs.
- Central Park has also been featured in 240 films, including *Stuart Little* (remember the boat scene?), *Breakfast at Tiffany's*, *Ghostbusters, Edward Scissorhands, Enchanted*, and *The Avengers*.
- The park is also home to a new species of centipede — *Nannarrup hoffmani*.

6

Chrysler Building

Among the towering skyscrapers in New York City, the Chrysler Building bows down to the Empire State Building, having lost its bragging rights of being called the world's tallest building to the Empire State Building after holding the distinction for a mere eleven months. The Chrysler Building was the World's tallest building at the time that it was built (1930), and The Empire State Building took over that distinction when it was completed in 1931.

Nowadays (2015), this Art Deco masterpiece, which was voted the top favorite building by Skyscraper Museum, is one of the tallest buildings in the city at 1,046 feet.

The Chrysler Building

This National Historic Landmark, named after its owner Walter Chrysler, is located at the intersection of Lexington Avenue and 42nd Street on the east side of Manhattan. It was designed by William Van Alen and took only two years to complete. The rush to finish the building was due to the then on-going competition to raise the highest skyscraper. In fact, the competition was so tight that the plans were kept secret to prevent other architects and builders from knowing the exact height the building would reach.

The Chrysler building is another popular setting for Hollywood movies? The Chrysler Building has made cameos in films such as *Spider-Man, Serendipity, My Super Ex-Girlfriend, Kate & Leopold,* and *The Devil Wears Prada*.

Fun Facts About the Chrysler Building

- More than 750 miles of electrical wire were utilized during the completion of the Chrysler building. That's like traveling from New York to Chicago!
- You can enjoy the view of New York City from any of the 3,862 windows on the building's façade.
- Since Chrysler is known for their automobiles, the building was riddled with decorations portraying car parts such as fenders and radiator caps. The eagle gargoyles are also reminders of Chrysler's involvement in the automobile industry. The gargoyle was once used as a hood ornament.

7

The Flatiron Building

There is a building in New York City called the Flatiron Building! It is called this because of its distinct triangular shape that resembles that of an actual flat clothes iron. Known previously as the Fuller Building (named after its original owner and founder George A Fuller), it is also sometimes called the "Cowcatcher" by locals.

Why "cowcatcher"? Well, there are many different stories out there, but just as the area that the building is built on was called "Flatiron" even before the building was built, the area was often referred to as "cowcatcher". Maybe because it was a small area between two busy roads and a good place for cows to be placed to keep them off the streets. This, of course, was at a time when people would actually have cows in town.

The building also has a small shop in the front. The shop is considered to be in the "cowcatcher" of the building as it looks a lot like the cowcatcher that is at the front of a train. Take a look at the next picture to see what I mean.

The cowcatcher on the Flatiron Building

Architect Daniel Burnham of Chicago designed the building to fit the triangular land allocated for the project. The Flatiron Building is located at the intersection of 23rd Street, Fifth Avenue, and Broadway. It is in front of the Madison Square Garden.

The Flatiron Building

While the Flatiron Building is one of the most iconic symbols of New York City, it had its share of criticisms during its construction. Many believed that the triangular shape of the building would not be stable enough to last. Others worried about the possible negative effects of its shape with regards to the wind tunnel effect. But that was more than 110 years ago, since the Flatiron Building was completed in 1902. Today, the Flatiron is still standing strong and has become one of the favorite spots in the city. It has been the subject of many photographs, paintings, and poems.

Fun Facts About The Flatiron Building

- The Flatiron Building isn't the first triangular structure built in the world. The Gooderham Building in Toronto, Canada and Atlanta's English-American Building beat the Flatiron by at least five years. The Ancient Egyptians got a head start as well, with some triangular temples and pyramids of their own.
- The building was supposed to have a giant clock face if Burnham's original sketches were followed? The US could have had its own Big Ben!
- The rooms at the pointy tip of the building measure six and a half feet wide. It is a lot smaller than what one would like to work in, but the view definitely makes up for it.
- Have you seen *Spider-Man*? The Daily Bugle, where Peter Parker worked, was housed in the Flatiron.
- Most true flatiron buildings are isosceles triangles. The flatiron building in New York City is actually a right triangle.

8

The Intrepid Museum

What's so different about this museum? Well, for one thing, it is called the Floating Museum. Science and history nuts will love this museum.

The Intrepid Museum is an actual aircraft carrier! The USS Intrepid served the United States during World War II and the Vietnam War. In between, it helped NASA recover things at sea. Sadly, the carrier was supposed to be destroyed - even after serving the country well, until a Good Samaritan came up with the idea of turning the majestic ship into a museum. Zachary Fisher fought to save the ship from being turned into scrap metal and succeeded. Thanks to Mr. Fisher, people can experience going inside an actual aircraft carrier while ogling at the many memorabilia stored in it.

The Intrepid Museum opened in 1982 and has since housed artifacts such as the Concorde Alpha-

Delta, an A-12 Blackbird spy plane, an F-14 Tomcat, a TBM Avenger torpedo bomber, a replica of the Aurora 7 capsule, and a host of personal memorabilia from many who served the country during the wars.

And…. there is also a submarine and a space shuttle there! The submarine USS Growler is situated right beside the Intrepid while the Space Shuttle Enterprise is safely tucked inside the Space Shuttle Pavilion. But that's not all! You'll certainly get a kick out of the navigation bridge, the rock-climbing wall, and the Transporter FX, a flight simulator.

Fun Facts About The Intrepid Museum

- The Concorde AD housed in the museum is the actual plane that broke records by flying in less than three hours across the Atlantic.
- The USS Growler (SSG 577) is the only submarine that is open to the public and which has actually fired nuclear missiles.
- The Enterprise is the first space shuttle orbiter ever built.

9

9/11 Memorial

A landmark in the United States that has a very tragic history is the 9/11 Memorial — constructed on the exact spot where the World Trade Center Towers once stood, where a total of 2,983 people died on that fateful day of September 11, 2001. In addition, it memorializes those who lost their lives during the 1993 World Trade Center bombing.

The National September 11 Memorial was designed by Michael Arad, while the landscaping was done by Peter Walker. The memorial was erected as a tribute to all the people who perished during two of the worst terrorist acts committed on American soil.

The 9/11 Memorial

The first people who had the privilege to visit the Memorial when it opened, were those who were present when the tragedy happened. A collection of survivors, responding authorities, and civilians who witnessed the attacks were invited to the opening on May 15, 2014. The memorial was then open to the public when it officially opened on May 21, 2014.

Some Facts About the 9/11 Memorial

- Donations from the private sector and public groups and individuals helped in constructing the $700-million 9/11 Memorial.
- Expecting a flow of emotions, tissues can be found everywhere in case they are needed. Exit doors can also be found in places where emotions are expected to run high. This is mainly to allow visitors to leave the premises if they don't want to be seen crying or anything to that effect.
- The Vesey Street Stair, or what is left of it, is now known as the "Survivor's Stairs". This is where hundreds of people passed through to escape the attacks. (What is left of the stairs are on display in the Museum – see the next chapter for a photo).

10

9/11 Memorial Museum

The September 11 Museum was dedicated on May 15, 2014 and opened to the public on May 21, 2014. The design was by Davis Brody Bond and the museum is about 70 feet below ground level. The museum is a 110,000 square foot publicly accessible space.

The museum has a deconstructive design to mirror the attacks on the buildings. There are two tridents from the Twin Towers that are still left standing after the attacks. Also, what is left of the Vesey Street Stair also known as "survivor staircase" is also located in the museum. Hundreds of people escaped the attacks of September 11 on those stairs.

The museum is designed to tell the story through narratives and displays of September 11, before, during, and after.

Located in the museum is Foundation Hall, where you will see a wall that is an exposed side of the slurry wall holding the Hudson River, as it remained unharmed during and after the September 11 attacks. There are other Ground Zero artifacts including pictures, personal effects, memorabilia, remembrance expressions, recorded testimonies, and first responder vehicles located in the museum. Every visitor to the museum has the opportunity to learn about the lives of every victim of the 2001 and 1993 attacks as they are commemorated in the museum.

Download the mobile app before going to the museum to enhance the experience. Remember, it is a place of remembrance and reflection when attending the museum.

Fun Facts about the Twin Towers and 9/11 Memorial Museum

- The World Trade Center, also known as the Twin Towers, opened on April 4, 1973. At completion of construction, these were the tallest buildings in the world. Each building was 110 stories tall.
- When visiting the museum, you can leave your own memory. You can tell your own 9/11 story or remember someone who was taken that September day. You can even add an opinion about some of the more challenging questions raised by 9/11. Your voice will be added to the audio archive and may be used for exhibits.

11

Times Square

New Year's Day is one of the biggest days for New Yorkers and tourists alike. Have you ever heard of the Times Square Ball? This one is no ordinary ball. The "Big Ball" measures twelve feet in diameter and weighs six tons! It's like one large elephant curled into a ball!

The world famous Ball Drop is an annual tradition that started in 1907 after former owner of The New York Times, Adolph Ochs, commissioned Artkraft Strauss to think of a better way to celebrate the New Year than just igniting fireworks. Since then, people of all ages, including kids like you, have flocked to Times Square to watch the yearly countdown.

Times Square is not only popular for the "Big Ball." It is actually more known for being one of the busiest intersections in the world. In fact, more than

335,000 people pass by the Square each day. Imagine that!

Times Square

Formerly known as Longacre Square, it is located in midtown Manhattan at the junction of Broadway and Seventh Avenue. This magical place got its current name after The New York Times transferred to the Times Building in April 1904. But did you realize that Times Square is not the only name it's known as? This brightly lit and bustling intersection is also called "The Crossroads of the World," "The Center of the Universe," "The Great White Way," and "The Tenderloin."

Once you reach this place "where all roads meet," your eyes will be bombarded with thousands of neon lights and numerous advertising billboards with dazzling designs. If you take the time to look down, you'll be greeted by superheroes, cartoon characters, Lady Liberties, and other personalities you normally only see on TV. However, if they're not your thing, you'll surely get a kick out of watching and listening to all the street performers and other artists all around Times Square.

Fun Facts About Time Square

- Numerous movies and TV shows have been filmed in Times Square. Tom Cruise seems to like the place so much that he has made two movies there — *Vanilla Sky* and *Jerry Maguire*. Tom Hanks' *Big*, particularly the scene where he played on a giant piano, was also filmed in Times Square.
- This popular tourist destination truly loves its visitors. Smoking has been prohibited in Times Square since 2011, allowing non-smokers and young people to enjoy the place even more.

12

Broadway Shows

Did you know that Broadway is actually an avenue? People hear the word so much when describing the shows that they often confuse Broadway as the theater or the shows themselves. When you hear the word Broadway, you imagine a place with bright lights, lots of music and dancing, and of course, fun!

The portion of Broadway, between 42nd and 53rd Streets is called "The Great White Way". Many think that is thanks to the many bright lights of the Theater District. But did you realize that before any of these theaters were put up, the stretch was already called "The Great White Way"? Since 1880, Brush arc lamps and, later on, electrical signs were placed along the stretch, making it one of the first illuminated streets in the country.

Did you realize that most of the theatres are found in places other than Broadway Avenue? Yep. Only four theaters are actually on Broadway Avenue; namely: The Marquis, The Palace, The Winter Garden, and The Broadway. Thirty-five other theaters are situated along 6th and 9th Avenues, while another is in Lincoln Center outside the Theater District.

Over twelve million people visit Broadway each year to catch the shows. Some of the most memorable shows to ever grace Broadway are *Cats, Miss Saigon, The Lion King, Les Miserable, The Phantom of the Opera,* and *Wicked*. Wicked stars Idina Menzel, the voice behind Elsa of Frozen.

Fun Facts About Broadway Shows

- The Tony Award is named after the former chairman and secretary of the American Theater Wing, Antoinette Perry. The first Antoinette Perry Award, a medallion with the iconic comedy and tragedy masks on one side and a silhouette of Perry on the other, was awarded in 1949. Two years prior to the current award, the group handed out a scroll and other memorabilia (a cigarette lighter or a compact) to the winners.

- The Phantom of the Opera holds the distinction of being the longest-running Broadway show ever. Andrew Lloyd Webber's masterpiece started its run on January 26, 1988, and is the only play on Broadway to celebrate its 18th – 25th anniversary on Broadway.

- The guy who killed Abraham Lincoln, John Wilkes Booth, is the brother of Edwin Booth who was one of the best actors ever to perform on Broadway. The Booth Theater is named after Edwin.

13

Grand Central Station

What's huge, has tons of people, and hides a lot of secrets? Oh, and there are lots of trains, as well. That's the Grand Central Terminal (GCT). The terminal is commonly mistaken as Grand Central Station, which is actually the name of the United States Post Office Station at 450 Lexington Avenue on the block adjacent to the GCT. People have become so used to using both names that they are now interchangeable.

The Grand Central Terminal opened on February 2, 1913 at exactly midnight. That means the GCT is over 100 years old! Not only is it one of the oldest, but it is THE largest train station on the planet. Did you know that the GCT has the highest number of platforms in the world, with a total of forty-four platforms that serve a total of sixty-seven tracks? Unbelievable, right? But the GCT needs all those platforms and tracks to help people get to where they're going. What do you think would happen if all 750,000 people who use the terminal have no other way to travel around New York? The city would probably be at a complete standstill if the GCT stopped working.

Grand Central Station

Now that you know how huge the terminal is and how many people pass through it every day, it's time to talk about its many secrets. Do you know that the terminal has a secret staircase? There is a hidden staircase that connects the atrium info kiosk to the lower concourse.

.

One of the most intriguing secrets the GCT has is what lies beneath the Waldorf-Astoria Building. Former US President Franklin D. Roosevelt used a secret platform under the building to hide the fact that he needed a wheelchair to get from one place to another.

Fun Facts About Grand Central Terminal

- The GCT can be seen in different movies such as *The Avengers, Madagascar, Madagascar: Escape 2 Africa,* and *Men In Black*.
- The oldest business operating in the GCT is the iconic Oyster Bar.
- The largest basement in NYC, measuring 49 acres, is located under the Main Concourse. It stretches from 42nd Street to 97th Street. It also has a secret room called M42, which is nowhere to be found in the GCT's blueprint.

14

The Brooklyn Bridge

Do you know which bridge was the first bridge ever to use steel-wire suspension? Yep, it's the Brooklyn Bridge. One of New York's most popular tourist destinations, the Brooklyn Bridge took fourteen years to build.

The Brooklyn Bridge spans 1,825 meters or about 6,100 feet. Do you think you could walk the entire 6,100 feet of the bridge? It would be a long walk but would probably be worth it because of the views. You can see such sights as the Statue of Liberty, the East River, the New York Harbor, and the Empire State Building from the bridge.

The Roebling family is, with little doubt, the most important group behind the building of the Brooklyn Bridge. John A. Roebling had the idea and designed the project. Unfortunately, he died of tetanus even before construction began, when his toes were crushed by a boat. His son, Washington, took over as chief engineer after his death. Washington later developed caissons disease and had to direct the completion of the bridge from his bed. His wife Emily acted as the liaison between Washington and the rest of the group involved in the project. Emily's contribution earned her the distinction of being "the first woman field engineer."

The Brooklyn Bridge

Fun Facts About The Brooklyn Bridge

- One type of bird that you will see flying above the Brooklyn Bridge is the peregrine falcons, touted the fastest animals alive. The peregrines, which can fly up to 200 miles per hour, have made the bridge their nesting site.
- The first person to jump from the bridge and reach the waters 135 feet below was swimming instructor Robert E. Odlum.
- If you've noticed the Brooklyn Bridge looks like the Golden Gate Bridge, it's because the Golden Gate Bridge was designed similar to the Brooklyn Bridge.

The Brooklyn Bridge

15

Coney Island

Coney Island is a neighborhood close to Brooklyn that is approximately a one-hour subway ride from downtown New York City. It has an amusement area that includes more than 50 rides and attractions.

Coney Island also has a boardwalk with beach access. There are restaurants and gift shops all along the boardwalk.

The main attraction of Coney Island is the rides. Below is a photo of Cyclone which is a wooden roller coaster left from the original Amusement Park – Astroland!

Coney Island

In addition to the rides, there is also a skating rink, an aquarium, bumper cars, and arcades.

Coney Island has a number of restaurants, and if you just want to snack on something while waiting for your turn on a ride, there are lots of kiosks and other food stalls. A not-to-be-missed restaurant is Nathan's Hot Dog Stand – the home of the National Hot Dog Eating Contest every July 4th!

Fun Facts About Coney Island

- Walt Disney once visited Coney Island to study how to run an amusement park. With many Disneylands all over the globe, Walt probably owes his success to Coney.
- The word "coney" means rabbit in Dutch. Rabbit-hunting was a popular sport and pastime during the early years of the island, hence the name.
- New York positioned itself as a possible venue for the 2012 Olympics. Then Mayor Michael Bloomberg envisioned a sports complex right in Coney Island. The plan fell through, though, after their bid was rejected.

16

Little Italy

Do you realize that there is a place in New York City where you can go to get a feel for what it's like to be in Italy?

Little Italy Subway Sign

Situated in Lower Manhattan, Little Italy is found smack in the middle of Canal and Houston Streets and Lafayette and the Browery. One of the best things about the place is the architecture. The buildings that stand there were built during the late 19th century or during the times of the early Italian settlers.

Food is one of the best reasons to visit — food is something that Italians are known for. Grab some authentic Italian dishes and pastries from any of the numerous restaurants that line up the place, especially along Mulberry Street.

Little Italy got its name after the Italians who travelled to America (mostly through Ellis Island) settled in this part of New York. Around 40,000 Italians were living in the area at the end of the 19th century.

A building in Little Italy

Fun Facts About Little Italy

- Nowadays, Little Italy is home to zero Italians who actually came from Italy and just a few American Italians still reside in the place.
- Mob families, prominent during the Prohibition era (1920-1933), have left Little Italy.
- Although the movie Godfather was set in Little Italy, there is actually no Corleone Family that ever lived there.

17

Chinatown

New York City's own Chinatown can be found at Manhattan's Lower East Side. It is right next to Little Italy, so a visit to that area will be a great way to learn and experience different cultures.

Chinatown Subway Sign

The earliest Chinese settlers in New York came here more than 150 years ago? Chinese immigrants came in droves to this specific area since 1860 to look for work or to do business. A few of them decided to settle in New York which eventually led to others to do the same. Today, up to 150,000 people from different countries live in Chinatown, including those from the Dominican Republic, Puerto Rico, and the Philippines.

For a long time, the Chinese settled in cramped houses with as many as fifteen people in a double-bedroom apartment. Today, Chinatown is one of New York's most visited tourist attractions, thanks to the number of Chinese restaurants, food carts, dumpling houses, bakeshops, trinket stores, and other attractions. The best time to visit Chinatown is during the Chinese New Year — that is, if you don't mind being in a huge crowd of people. The festive atmosphere of the parade will surely help you forget the crowd as long as you stay close to your mom and dad.

Shopping in Chinatown

Aside from the food and festivities, Chinatown is known for its traditional tea shops, and lots of stores that sell herbs and spices. Do you like ice cream? Then go to the Original Chinatown Ice Cream Factory and sample as many ice cream flavors as you want.

Other places to see in Chinatown include the Museum of the Chinese in the Americas, the Lin Zexu statue, the Mahayna Buddhist Temple, and the Eastern States Buddhist Temple.

Fun Facts About Chinatown

- You can take a tour which guides you to places in Chinatown that appeared in several Hollywood films such as *What a Girl Wants* and *The Amazing Spider-Man 2*.
- The TV series *Gotham*, which tells the story of a younger Bruce Wayne and Jim Gordon, is filmed in Chinatown.

18

Shopping on Canal Street

Looking for a bit of shopping? Head on over to Canal Street, that crazy shopping hub in the midst of Manhattan's eclectic Chinatown and check out the massive and varied selection of souvenir items, accessories, clothes, bags, toys, novelty art, and knickknacks of every kind.

Pearl River Mart

Step inside the Pearl River Mart and you won't believe how many inexpensive but totally awesome things you can buy! Do you like Hello Kitty? This store is filled with Hello Kitty clothes, slippers, stuffed toys, lamps, and costumes! Get paper lanterns and Chinese dolls for your room. Check out the Buddha statues and jade jewelry for your parents. Have you ever seen an inflatable cat in a can? Or a glittery, golden, ceramic pig with a moving tail? Get these and more at this fun store on the border of Broadway and SoHo.

Shopping on Canal Street

Yunhong Chopsticks Shop

Of course, you can't visit Chinatown without getting souvenir chopsticks! At this colorful shop, you'll see hundreds of different kinds of chopsticks made from a range of materials and printed with faces, flowers, animals, and other designs. You can get chopsticks painted with famous works of art and even chopsticks that depict your birth year!

Open-air vendors

Canal Street is famous for the amazing number of vendors selling items such as makeup, bags, watches, perfume, hats, exotic fruits and vegetables, and even jewelry. Walk through this area, especially between Mulberry and Broadway, from Mulberry to the Bowery, and around the corner to Grand Street, and you'll surely find something you'll want to take home.

Fun Facts about New York's Canal Street

- Can you guess how Canal Street got its name? Well, before Canal Street was a street, it was a canal. And before there was a canal, there was a small body of water called Collect Pond where New Yorkers would hang out during the warmer months. Eventually, the pond got too polluted and a canal was dug to drain the water out. That canal was then covered up and later became Canal Street.
- Canal Street is the main route that connects New Jersey and Brooklyn.
- Canal Street is the center of Chinese jewelry shopping in Chinatown.

19

The New York City Subway

The New York City Subway will take you to the most interesting places in the city. Are you up for a trip to Coney Island? How about seeing some penguins, sea lions, and beluga whales? Then ride the subway and make a stop at West 8th Street. Want to see some dinosaurs? Take the D line and get off at 81st Street to visit the Museum of Natural History. If you want to see some live animals, get off at Eastern Parkway and head to the Prospect Park Zoo.

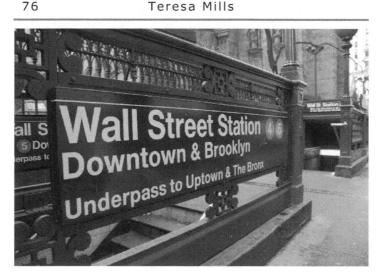

One entrance to the Subway

The New York City Subway is one of the easiest ways to get around the city, and it is the busiest Rapid Transit System in the United States (It is one of the busiest in the world).

The subway system runs through Manhattan, as well as Queens, Brooklyn, and the Bronx (4 of the 5 boroughs). So, you can literally get almost anywhere in the area on the subway system.

Construction on the NYC subway system started in 1900. The system opened officially in 1904. Nearly 9 million people ride the NYC subway system each workday and over 2.5 billion use it each year! Wow!!!

The Interior of the Subway

Fun Facts About The NYC Subway

- The Times Square subway stop is the busiest in the NYC subway system.
- Dispatchers avoid letting a train leave from Pelham Bay Park at 1:23 p.m. Yep, it's because of the film *The Taking of Pelham 123*.
- The entire length of the NYC subway system is over 660 miles.
- When the system opened in 1904 there were less than 30 stops. Today there are more than 450 stops.

I hope you enjoyed visiting New York City. Next let's head southeast to Washington DC where we will learn about US currency and find out about the strange shape of the Washington Monument!

https://kid-friendly-family-vacations.com/booktour-visitwdc

Sign up for my newsletter for all upcoming updates as well as some free gifts.

https://kid-friendly-family-vacations.com/nycattractions

Are you ready to visit Europe? Let's fly to Paris, France where we will learn about a resting place for human bones under the city and about a mummy haunting a museum!

https://kid-friendly-family-vacations.com/booktour-visitparis

---

Learn more about the entire Hey Kids! Let's Visit series!

https://kid-friendly-family-vacations.com/booktour-series

Please leave a review to help others lean more about New York City whether traveling or learning from home.

https://kid-friendly-family-vacations.com/review-nyc

MORE FROM KID FRIENDLY FAMILY VACATIONS

BOOKS

Books to help build your kids / grandkids life experiences through travel and learning

https://kid-friendly-family-vacations.com/books

COLORING AND ACTIVITY PAGKAGES

Coloring pages, activity books, printable travel journals, and more in our Etsy shop

https://kid-friendly-family-vacations.com/etsy

RESOURCES FOR TEACHERS

Resources for teachers on Teachers Pay Teachers

https://kid-friendly-family-vacations.com/tpt

It is our mission to help you build your children's and grand-children's life experiences through travel. Not just traveling with your kids... building their "Life Experiences"! Join our community here: https://kid-friendly-family-vacations.com/join

Acknowledgments

Proof-reading / Editing
Marcia Reagan at Proof-Raider.com

Cover Photos
NYC Skyline - © rabbit75_dep/ deposit photos

Brooklyn Bridge – © sepavone / deposit photos

Cheesecake - personal vacation photo

Statue of Liberty – © masteriu / deposit photos

Photos in Book
Empire State Building - © ventdusud / deposit photos

Statue of Liberty – 2 photos from personal vacations

Rockefeller Center - © Kittiwarang Kitipong-pithaya/123rf.com

Rockefeller Center Tree - © gary718 /123rf.com

Top of the Rock Observatory – ©brezina123 /123rf.com

Central Park - © Songquan Deng / 123rf.com

Central Park (Angels of the Waters) - © Carlos Neto / 123rf.com

Chrysler Building - ©Richard Semik /123rf.com

ABOUT THE AUTHOR

Teresa Mills is the bestselling author of the "Hey Kids! Let's Visit..." Book Series for Kids!

Teresa's goal through her books and website is to help parents / grand-parents who want to build the life experiences of their children / grand-children through travel and learning activities.

She is an active mother and Mimi. She and her family love traveling in the USA, and internationally too! They love exploring new places, eating cool foods, and having yet another adventure as a family! With the Mills, it's all about traveling as family.

In addition to traveling, Teresa enjoys reading, hiking, biking, and helping others.

Join in the fun at kid-friendly-family-vacations.com

Made in the USA
Monee, IL
23 May 2022